I0412505

The Unbound Heart

David R. Frey

Virginia Beach, Virginia

© 2011 by Createspace

All rights reserved.
ISBN-13:978-1461190639

LCCN

Printed in the United States of America.

This book is for the many people in the world that long to have meaningful relationships with friends and partners. Those that may also struggle to find a deeper sense of self in life long goals.

Special thanks to my loving wife Melissa, without her being in my life I would not be the man that I am today. Her love and compassion for me has given me purpose that is much greater than I could have ever dreamed.

Thanks to my mother, always being there and supporting me through every day.

Thanks to my mother-in-law Bonnie, who has helped me in reaching newer rationality and to seek having many deep conversations of the heart.

Contents

Where in life do we find ourselves? Always a great journey that can lead us to familiar waters or great adventures in an open world or right back to home again. It's always said that life's greatest mystery is that to which we find our own love, our own heart and our own mind. I would be fooling myself if I knew all the answers or had been down every street for there are many that I have not travelled yet either. In truth, there is a great adventure of my own that I am traveling and learning from. So in writing this for you and it would be a pleasure if we would be real with each other in hopes to guide one another.

1

Home

Where is your home? Is this an actual place that you find yourself in constantly and just refer to it as home? When finding oneself in the shoes of another is just a common way of seeing the light breaking through a double pane window. There is a continuous sheen of echoes that follow everyone and of that what we have experienced from others or life stories that makes us feel this is our home or the place to be. "I go to work and come home"- so blunt and empty that it becomes just a characteristic of state, not a feeling or belief of where home truly is. When you find yourself longing to be exactly where your heart intends you to be then you will know that you have arrived home. "The home is where the heart is" such a statement that expands the truth, the way your heart expresses its joys and its happiness in waking each and every day to a place that gives you warmth and comfort. Seeing the people you want to see with open arms and playful laughter, where tears of sorrow and joy are shared commonly knowing there is nothing better. For many years I never had a home, that to which was a true home; just had the mental space of coming and going with a place to stay. The unraveling of a tormented heart had pushed me from the world I was born into and bore the weight of undying pain. It took lots of searching, seeking and travels to finally find where my home is. Sometimes this isn't even a place, the home can be many things but all of which bring true tidings of love, where your heart resides and exists freely with the sunrise and setting upon the soul. Some days it may be that you find yourself without meaning or purpose draining you but it is in our home that we find our way and passion; giving light to every new emersion or adventure we take. If by no means allow this warmth to leave your heart, grab hold of this and care oh so tenderly for our home is very precious and meant to be as much of a dream as it should be a reality. Many of people go through each day without knowing of their own home's worth, appreciate what grace we have for many have lost before us. There are lots of fantasies that tell stories of countryside and palaces and glorious happy ever after, why though would you look to live a made up story then instead of writing your own true one? I have asked myself what I should write for years as many of friends have waited for me to actually put down my thoughts. Many of short crappy blurbs were produced along the way, probably because always has there been the mindset to give consideration or the reasoning of life long expectancy but nevertheless people fail somehow and meaning is lost. It's not reality that causes the dismay or dissolution of man, but the people within the world that are unfair, unreasoning or not thoughtful that affect the environments that we go through. Finding your home amongst the many tragedies is not an easy task by any means, even myself, I feel I have found where my home is but as of right now I am alone in it. Not that I am lonely or lonesome, but that the person whom I share my life with is not here and I have failed to completely grasp that she isn't gone but doing as is necessary. Things may happen or lead a course that was unforeseen, but always remember that your own heart is very strong in that it provides you oxygen to move yourself forward through each day continuing in action. Home, it's where you want to be in the end of each day. Mine is in the arms of the one that I truly love. If you find your home the same as I then it should be asked of yourself what you see when you look at their pictures, when you see their face, when you hear their laughter. It should be overwhelming with emotion, not even that which words can truly describe. Of course we are human so we try our best to say what we are feeling or seeing or hearing… this is just nature toying with us, antagonizing us to put words to something that is indefinable. I have found myself in the eyes of many of other women for one reason or another, and yet it doesn't matter because I have found my home through my wife, it's even a struggle to pay attention to another as though the room is quiet when being spoken too. This is kind of fascinating seeing as attention is that which we all desire in some form or fashion, but it is so much more than the attention that should be desired. Who cares what you look like today or tomorrow, if you shaved or didn't- does it even matter? It shouldn't really even be of concern; I know waking in the place I call home I am loved for as I am. Truly there is nothing better than the love and admiration shared in a good home. Always is it better to see that which we are as people and as self to be blessed with such a cherished home.

2

Self Worth

So where should we go then from here, down the spiraling adventure we call love? Not yet, there is much to talk about before we get to that. Self worth, sounds like a good place to cross paths with so let us describe this then. This is your own mental status quo; no one else should ever play a part in your view self worth. Sometimes this can be hard to do right? Society has been brought up to believe that what you see on TV, or in magazines is how we should judge ourselves in the grander scheme. If we aren't loaded to the top with money, fashion, and makeup or have the body of a Greek god/goddess, then we aren't equal amongst one another. Sorry, but not everyone will be like that, there are some that do benefit well in some of these aspects… most of them have paid high dollar for those looks or that hair or those clothes. Don't get me wrong I love a nice suit and tie and luxury that sometimes I really cannot afford, but that's just how we set our standards in our life, this has nothing to do with your self worth. A question I like to ask is "when you look in the mirror, what do you see?" the response that I would love to hear but never do is "a great gift". A present that has been given to life and maybe to someone else; without any cause for looking at how you ended up where you are, that you are still very special and always will be. Sadly, life is sometimes lost before given the chance to even see them self in the mirror of life, to even give a moment of consideration in this world. I am sorry to those that have had such a gift lost; there are no words describing your pain or loss. This is never an easy trial that some face yet even facing such heartache you are still blessed with opportunity as well to see the beauty in yourself and others. Thankfully I am very fortunate to have three beautiful children, healthy and strong, one day have maybe their own to where our family continues to grow; god willing if there is a loss of such, that we will comfort one another as a family and show greatness to our gifts.   Everyone has there own thing that they think is part of their self worth, 'oh, I look fat' or 'damn, I need to shave" or what not... these are just the outlines. Tell yourself the truth, and believe it, that you are amazingly special to life itself. That the world is nothing more than a foothold that you are conquering each step of the day no matter how random it can be. How much more is there to see, what should be said is that you love yourself for you. I know for a fact that there is someone that will love you in the same way and tell you words that you long to hear without even thinking about it; however you need to believe them as well and truly see it. In light of this there isn't a redemption of yourself pride for anything you have done, there is only forgiveness of yourself. If for some reason you have fallen in to where you feel the lesser for this, then it is you that has to forgive yourself no matter how much the thought of someone else forgiving you may seem real. This ties heavily into your self worth, because when you are looking through a window instead of seeing the reflection then how do others see you as well? We all get down in the dumps; it's bound to happen sometime in your life. Not that I wish you anything negative, don't take me wrong, but it seems to just happens somehow. Here is where all the practice and the times that you have given meaning to yourself and to the person in the mirror truly matter. Where do you go from this? The sun, find your way to feel the warmth, this is not a literal statement, what I am saying is find your sunshine and bask in its radiance. Days are not meaningless at all; there is always some meaning in what is going on or how things happen but may just seem irrelevant to you. I know I am stressing self worth a lot, because I am still judging my own self and making changes that need to happen in my life, yet none of these though have made my own picture of self any less just needing fine tuning. It is that which we believe whole heartedly to be true that contains the keys to our lives. Sound stupid? Maybe it might be, but who is to say that anyone wouldn't love arriving at anywhere with the thoughts that you are the best of the best and no one around is better or ever will be. Definitive of true self worth.

3

Pictures of Reality

So the pictures on the wall or that you carry speak of your life as it has gone through many changes. You used to be thin, or ugly, or even beautiful in them, right? Get out of town, they are just pictures, snap shots that show our life story, that we look back upon and either love or hate. Don't make them seem more than that; admire what is in them for the time you had, or the craziness of life's whatever's. People always show me pictures and then they glance at my face to see my reaction. Yes, I can see beauty or not so pretty, or whatever to describe the photo itself, but what do you want me to know about that moment? I wasn't there, so please tell me the story to share your emotion based in that photo. Pictures are worth a thousand words, but never are they the same for everyone? I love hearing my wife describe events that happened in the photos she has from her youth, she remembers so much of the things that have taken place and I can feel her emotion from them. Looking at my own photos taken of me or by me I can also tell you a lifetime of things, here is when a real reaction comes forth and gives much greater meaning. I like paintings too, I hate the Mona Lisa… what in the hell is wrong with her? Is she happy, sad, melancholy, it's always been a mystery to anyone who looks at it; yes, it is quite lovely a painting, very exquisite in it's artistic form but is it her then that we are seeing or just the painting itself. This is how we know that life is real, by seeing into the photos and depicting the life, the love, the joys, the sorrow, the hurt. Each one of us bases our reality in an emerald dream, kind of like Dorothy finding the emerald city right. No silly, this is our life, the one we build, and develop from the ground up. It isn't fair to say that there is no picture that has any meaning in it or to it, but those involved that it has reference too. My wife and I love taking photos of our lives, especially our children, times when they are being off the wall or just relaxing with each other. Our moments to which we can look back upon and share our love for what we have together and the undefined joys. It should be known to never displace someone else's reality to a simple definition, I think it is exceptional to be in a photo, taking one or part of a moment in someone's life no matter what or where it is. Can be a basis of our consideration for love itself to which provides us with unrestrained glory in the endearment of others. Ah, amoré. They are just samples of that to which we are seeking, pieces of a puzzle that compliment each other in building a solid structure. So take many photos of your life, yourself, the people you see around you and remember those moments as they truly bare meaning to you and serve to acknowledge so many wonders around us.

Honesty

Being honest is very hard to do all of the time, sometimes it may seem as though the truth will be more hurtful than skipping past with a lie. I know many of people that have told me that I am too honest and open about everything, yet interestingly enough they seem to always come back and tell me thank you at a later time for whatever reason that we had a discussion to begin with. I should probably clarify something because a lot time's people mistake the defining an act or if acting as a certain way is not the same as a direct statement to or about someone. Yes, sometimes things hurt to say to some-one, especially if they take it the wrong way; even more importantly towards someone you care for. "I can't say that to him or he will get angry and freak out." – How do you really know this is always the case? There was a book that I read a few times called *The 5 Love Languages* by Gary Chapman; in there he talks about different situations and how to address circumstances differently. Do I think they will work for eve-ryone? I don't believe that everyone has a curvature that can be aligned to not have an issue of some sort; but knowing at least some foundation on how to represent what you are trying to say is that much better in the end. My mother in law taught me that I sound totally different in person then when I write something down, so I am working on that too. Unfortunately there are some people that are complete sociopaths and have no real feelings of remorse or consideration for life itself then you will be heard, but wont matter anyway. Immediate re-sponses are always going to be as the presentation is displayed for them, writing being the lowest form, then phone, then person. Always remember, "For every action there is a reaction." –Newton's Law of physics describes this in a chemical and material composition but this is easily shown through normal people fairly easily. If I spit on someone they are going to get mad, upset, maybe embarrassed; the same is said for hugging someone. Recently, I walked up to an elderly lady, and I never met her before, carried her bags to her car for her then leaned over slowly and gave her a great big bear hug. She started crying, but not of sorrow, she looked at me and said, "No one has hugged like that in a long time, is there a reason why you did?" Her honesty hit me heavily as it took me a minute to respond because of my own issues that I am facing almost wallowed from anguish and hurt, but I looked at her and said "There was no reason, you look very nice and I hope you have a wonderful day." She smiled at me and I walked away; I don't actually know her story but she smiled and for that moment she seemed fairly happy. There is no amount of response that may come, from the greatest joys to the most horrendous arguments, but the intelligence that we have as people, grown through experiences is how we are going to make differences in that which we do. I have a temper, I have always had a temper, everyone has always hated my reactions when my emotions let loose. Not so much a physical side where sadly it is having the tongue of a pit viper, fast and painstaking. Through many a years I have struggled with this problem, I have isolated my four biggest issues and now am upholding them because they are most important to me in not allowing the inner fire to burn hotter. Everyone will have their own lists of things that upset them, and if they say nothing upsets them, then they are either lying or fooling themselves. It is impor- tant to know the things that make you upset because if you don't acknowledge them they will scorch you for the rest of your life. Mine are actually pretty simple from an outlook of morality: No cheating, don't lie, don't steal, and fairly re- cently I came to my fourth which is a little less straight forward but it's almost general to everyone cause at some point they will feel the same way. This is: I am not stupid, I may not understand fully right now what is going on or happening, please warden me some time to have a better response for both of us. Am sure when you go to the supermarket and want to buy something and a clerk is busy stocking shelves and you ask them a question with no response, it is hard to not be like "hey you! Answer me right now! It's your job!" Yes it is their job to help you out, but here is that time thing, relax, you may be in a hurry to do something else but they may be as well. This concept sometimes isn't easy for the other person to get which is ok, but here I am being honest with you in hopes that you also can be honest with yourself and others. Don't be thoughtless in your own actions or words and then expect for someone else to not be thoughtless as well, reactions are all based upon that initial action, display, or conversation. So if you can possibly go through each day being honest with yourself and those around you then there are no need for anything more than just simple conversions. Life would be so much simpler if this was how everyone understood each other or related information but one can only hope to always get the straightforward truth all the time.

5

Moral Fibers

Ah yes, with honesty comes morality… almost as a social outcast nowadays with all the TV shows and news articles that give no bearing to how to survive in real life without being looked down upon or shamed. So much promotion for immoral acts it's almost as though life itself has become one great big piss-hole of deception and horrible display of the soulless. Not trying to be religious by any means here, but I have read many of theological books; even in real paganism, which is the worship of women, there is time of fruitfulness and time of life giving. They sound the same right? In actuality, they are quite different in that, yes there is a time of no thought, letting loose of and being a destructive force in ones self which brings forth the time of embodiment; the time at which you have grown to adulthood and now the fruits of your labor and life bare love, home and family. Everyone goes through this within their lifetime, some people let loose a little earlier in life, whimsical and unbound; others a little later in life depending on where you happen to be at that point in your growth. It's not a bad thing to learn from, hopefully you haven't found yourself as one of the less than fortunate through this. I must clarify because I am not looking down just saying that sometimes shit happens, and by less than fortunate I do mean found with an incurable disease, a horrible memory of being drugged, raped, beaten or an unplanned pregnancy (having a child from a night of inhibitions). If these happened to you I am so sorry, if it has hurt you to remember then to take any of the pains away I would. The topic doesn't change with reason to the down side of things; there are good fun times that can occur from letting loose a little bit, meeting new people, finding out you can do nine shots of straight Everclear, or other enjoyments. In thinking on these experiences there are times when you need to definitely realize the importance of what's around you though, are you a mother, a father, a husband, or a wife, do others depend on you as being stable and firm in reality and if so then learn from what you have enjoyed and define yourself. If you are that important to someone then would you be willing to sell yourself short as just a party ticket instead of just sharing in some laughter? I do know that I would not trade being a husband and father for a night of debauchery. Just cause you watch or have knowledge of others that have unclean acts does not make it any less demeaning of your character, I can state this statement with perfect knowledge of how I felt of myself when I had affairs on my first wife. She forgave me quickly but I didn't love her as a man should love his spouse, truly I did not have feelings for her that I have now for my wife now of real love and caring. We have reconciled as friends and in our conversations she has told me that my new wife is very fortunate, and even with the arguments or issues we had; my first wife tells me that I am a really good man. Very deafening. The very thought that with my immoral acts and some unrestrained words that hurt her, she can tell me that I am a good man, and a great father. Sometimes we as people live a thousand life times in one life, we see things in that very moment or other times in recollection of past events, but no matter what we do there will always be an opinion not of our own but from someone that has cared for us. Even in facing new trials or occurrences, reflecting and matching the heart to the mind is not always so easy to do. It would be a walk in the park on a Sunday afternoon if we all could just say, "fuck that, fuck you, and fuck this…" to just walk away without ever a thought or care for the person or people around us or in our lives. In that we are human beings, we have surpassed to be-ing just an animal through having emotions. You may not feel or see the direct impact now or in that moment for your own acts but there will be a time when you do remember, when you do hear that which may you may or may not wish to hear. So decide what is good and evil, and hopefully ones own morality aids in following the right path.

_6_

Grasping All of Life

Embodiment of life, you're probably sitting there wondering what the hell am I talking about? Yes, me too sometimes… no, in all honesty, I am talking about today. Today, I woke up, got dressed and went to work. Ugh, so bland; how about reference to I woke up this morning and saw pictures of my darling wife which instantly filled my heart with joy for the wonderful things we have shared in our lives. I put some nice clothes and checked myself out real quick in the mirror "damn I am sexy", told myself in thought. Hung out for a minute with the dog and kitty before hoping in my truck and cruising off singing and listening to beats on the radio. That is defining, not saying you should be so descriptive, we all have our own way of saying something; but to know what's going on to you, to that around you, to the life that exists everywhere. Stopping several times to help others stuck in snow banks get unstuck, they don't know me, they don't know I am a complete asshole; but I see them and wish to give them assistance as best I can. I came across a mother of 5, standing outside her run down minivan crying, she was out of gas and looking for assistance of any kind. I asked if I could help, I could see the in her face her desperation as no one stopped, no one looked, so I filled her gas tank. Her oldest son of maybe 6 liked football, was tossing it around a little bit and had a beat down old jersey. As the woman crying with joy thanking me for helping, I looked at the boy and told him that if he loves the game and is persistent, it will embrace him. I didn't say anything to the lady aside from "I hope you make it home safe." She said many a blessings and gave me praise;

but I am not special by helping someone; it really is seeing life as a whole and being certain to give one another care. I did cry when I left, for my wife is very far from me, but she has helped me so much in realizing that to embody life altogether is to love fully and be thankful for each and every day that we have together in the walk of life. I only talked a lot of these two things that I have done, because the meaning to me is so much different then that of what it is to those needing aid. Knowing that each day is important, that all the joys, the sorrows, and in betweens have meaning; a purpose, and it may not even be for you; it may be something for someone else to find or see that you are just helping their path. Do not dispose of the lives around you or plague them with hurtful thinking, there are warmongers like me to do that for you. In visiting a hospital near Monado, Indonesia, it was different. It was beautiful for it was horrendous, you may not understand this as I say it. So blood is everywhere, people aligned the walls, feces smell through the air, and some very jarring sights; but in the vision of a nightmare the people were getting helped, it wasn't fast and am sure the system could have worked better had they been more modernized, but for what they have available they lived. They carried on to the next day, eventually they maybe able to fix everyone that was in there for their injuries and of course there may have been some loss. In those moments where everything around you reaches for life, is when life truly embraces us; and we make the decisions that follow to embrace it back. Embodiment of your life is a project that we continually develop and work toward correcting in some way. Not so hard is a day to take time and walk in someone else's shoes, and see what life means to them. It may bring to you a challenge of creating a world that has a different meaning, where life is of purity. Bare witness to a child playing, laughing, singing, and see the world as such an joy as to not give away.

7

Selfish?

Selflessness… oh yes, I have been told that I am selfish in my thinking, usually this point seems to only happen when I am reacting to something or enraged; well no kidding. I can honestly say that I too am my own worse enemy here, where when upset or hurt I have acted selfishly. Even still it is interesting to me that if you devote every day and everything that you are as a person to provide love and care for others that you are now selfish in your agitation. When you go through your life seeing the world as a whole and try to understand the ways of the people that revolve around you are transpiring in then you aren't really selfish. It's easily misconstrued that when emotions are being kicked around for whatever reason that you may act selfishly in that state of being. So love your partner or spouse, your children, your pets, your friends; not that you don't love them, but through your day think of them as what would they wish. You may not want to eat at Outback and want Burger King… compromise with each other, think to why they may want that instead, maybe they want to sit down with you and enjoy a nice meal together rather than just riding through the pick up window. Now, can't just agree to everything with a child's desire, otherwise we'd be eating McDonald's almost every meal; but understand that they have a thought too, their own completion for enjoying the day. Try the park it's wonderful to step outside and enjoy the day, oh my god fresh air, blech. Seriously though, if your own thoughts get you through a day, but you consider those of others and the things around into all your decisions then you lose selfishness and make way yourself ready for a new level of existence. Someone will always tell you that you are being selfish, ok, if you know that you are giving your all to listen, compromise, and plan together; then maybe you have been selfish for a moment, but on a broader scale this is not true.

Wrongful Desires

Who doesn't like pizza every once in a while? Mmmm, so delicious. Where in the world would we be without it? The same holds true for lots of things, especially lust. The rearing head of lust comes about with an infatuation for something or someone. Whether it is an item, money, a characteristic, or sex. This damn thing is by far the biggest troublemaker in everyone's lives and can even be pinpointed by some easily. I don't care what your fancy is; everyone creates a lusting in some way or fashion. Mine happens to be cars and clothes, would be nice to have the fastest and sexiest car on the street and be dressed in the best attire around. Mine thankfully is of the lesser side where I just don't have the funds that I would like right now to be able to get these things. This only becomes a very hurtful thing when we find ourselves lusting for something to which we may not have or maybe shouldn't have or do at all. I have watched several of my friends go down the path of lust in the sexual manner, leaving inhibitions of their wives and children for that sexy chick on the boardwalk that spreads herself for the next best thing that walks her way. The downfall for them was tremendous, loss of careers, so many a broken hearts, and sadly has ruined lives of people that should matter most to them. The moment when their lust had taken over them uncontrollably should have been the moment that they haltered and regained their wits about them to see their own demise. It's not just the idea, or the mind messing with us; its like that old saying the grass is always greener, for them it sure was not by any means. It is in the act of lust where we fail as having common sense, today I can't go buy a Lamborghini, I sure as hell want one, but if I act upon that, we would be bankrupt tomorrow mid-afternoon. Then we'd lose everything for no reason but to just have a few moments in something to dream for. It's ok to think, damn I want that, damn that's nice, or for the promiscuous- damn I want that booty. At this moment in your thinking STOP. Really think about all the possibilities that can happen, about all the things that you could affect or destroy. Is it really worth it? If you are carefree and have no control of yourself at all then you probably deserve what happens as the after effect. If I walk to a dealership with the intent on buying that hotrod I still have a choice, when the papers are being prepared, I don't have to sign. It is good thing that as people we have rea-soning that doesn't have to let lust control us. I know some people would argue that, 'oh, I was just doing it do it" or "I wanted it." Right on, that's all you; you take what you want don't be surprised later on... Sometimes this works out to our benefit as well though, for instance, I love my wife, I adore her deeply, but I do lust for actively. This is a good thing only in the respect that to me she is extremely gorgeous and sexy. Am sure they may be other people don't see her the same as I do, but that's ok because to me she is. So hopefully be aware of that which you are lusting for and understand that whatever it may be, you need to think of how your life may turn to or away from it.

9

Ability to Answer

Questionability is an awkward word to say but so are some questions when being asked. Having a keen sense that there is going to be a question as to why, what, or when just means that you are going to expect to be questioned. We aren't always good at stating questions and have to rephrase or correct ourselves in this way too, but everyone has questions some more than others. I love multiple choice questions, A,B,C,D.... you know two of the answers are wrong pretty much from the get go and then can make an educated decision based on the other two. Not always that way and then there may be a description part. If you have never had to answer a question then how do know that you have even thought about something or learned anything at all? Sometimes the answers we give or receive are very straight forward, sometimes very shadowed with illusion; but if you never ask then you never know. I have been typing my questions lately before I ask especially if it's something important. This is to help me better ask the question seeing as being intelligent doesn't mean that we are always smart in the way we talk. Don't be scared to give an answer, to reply to what it is they are asking. Don't be scared to ask a question, you may need to know. I ran into this a little while back, I had asked a few friends of a friend if they have heard from him with responses of no. I finally was able to reach his mother, she cried and told me he had passed in an accident. It pained me a lot to hear, I sent her flowers and visited his burial. Sometimes life gives us the worst answers in the world. The question of how you as a person are is going to mean something in your lifetime.

10

Misdirection

"What the eyes see and the ears hear the mind believes" – John Travolta *Swordfish*. Interesting line where he refers to misdirection. We often do this in our lives to lead others away from something that we feel might hurt us or hurt them in some manner of respect. It's like feeling that there may be a different outcome from what was intended or desired originally so as to bypass some time we give undefined meaning to ascertain a different way to approach things. How can someone say they are being honest if they are being misleading;

they can't really but as long as it's not a straight forward lie then it might just need to be that moment of breathe they need to catch before they say what they need to say to you. I don't know for sure cause knowledge is not something that I would like to keep from anyone especially if it is a means to something that might help him or her out, whether it is a job or an entitlement. Try to be willing to give the straightforward answer instead of misdirecting them no matter how hard it may seem you would like not to. It sucks being on the receiving end of this diversion trying to wait for a real reason to come about while being patient or understand why it took place to begin with. It is human nature to have great expectations and hopefully see the results that we wish would be the best. So if for whatever reason you feel you are being misled, just breathe for a few minutes and hopefully the person or persons will give you better clarity at another time.

11

Controlling

Control, this comes in many different forms from controlling ones self to controlling a situation to controlling someone else. Many times this is referred to as the burden, which we have to carry to be socially acceptable; well yes, you don't just run around in public naked and not expect people to think you belong in a Looney bin. So having positive control over yourself is a good thing, especially if emotionally torn apart or having the mindset of losing ones self; it is by our own control that we can try to maintain a level of decency or restraint. I personally struggle with this one because I have let my emotions get the best of me when I am overwhelmed. This is something we all have to work on to an extent to maintain balance and clear positive reasoning. Controlling a situation can be just as hard by the way of how things are happening and how things are going about being conducted. Someone else may be ramped up and throwing carelessness into the wind where you are trying to maintain ideology of the situation and the two collide like fire and ice… This is where a compromise of some sort plays a part in obtaining a specific goal. So readjust to the situation and accomplish it as a partnership, or team. Now, the controlling of someone else; don't lie to yourself and say you have never tried to do this cause we all have in one-way or another. Whether it is through simple telling someone as your will to bribing someone with that they might want or need. No one can say that they have never done this, it's like they are giving themselves reason to do it continuously. However, if you are on the receiving end of what you feel is controlling then take a second to see what the other person is trying to control because maybe it's just a desire to reach out to you and they maybe don't know the best way to do so? I know it sounds silly, but there are times that I have been accused of controlling when really I am just trying to see what in the world is going on and in trying to understand have made own logic pertinent. This is different for everyone, some people really just don't know where their limitations are and then you have to reconsider the possibility that they are dumbfounded to their own acts of controlling. Never know; communication is a great thing.

12

Individualism

After the fact of knowing where you should be when it comes to control there most definitely comes the fact of individuality. From birth we are all given our own traits and comes with this our own way of being ones self or acting. Through growth we will follow many a trends that others have been laid out such as education, clothing designs, and the picturesque of ourselves in others eyes. Yet we always maintain our own sense of individuality, and how we perceive yourself and the life around us, the more common term would be our own vanity. It is not vain to have your own individualization but to recognize who you are and where you come from is how we separate ourselves from our peers that are proven to be most important. It's being Dionysian in an Apollonian run universe, where we have free thought and concepts of life under the rule of governments created in or before our time. Having the mindset that you are an individual should not be a part of how your relationship is or should be going though. Being the individual you are has given you relationships and made you parts of other peoples lives in one-way or another. This constantly is a reminder that we are accepted by the outside world no matter how dramatic a case may be for ones individualism. I have been the most cruel and difficult person that I know; having endured a tormenting past has made me fairly cold-hearted; yet I have a very soft and loving side as well. I am very much an individual in life itself. I have many friends and people that love me as I am for even with having negative traits; they have all said that I am the best friend that anyone could ever have. So is said that when you see yourself in your own mind understand what makes you an individual, if you have issues with yourself then work progressively to fix them but always know that you are loved for the person you truly are. Yes, don't expect people to not point out your negativities or mistakes, cause they are trying to help you learn to be a better influence in society and in those around you; this should not take away from your individuality by any means but to help you grow in your social responsibilities and acceptance. Being a sole survivor is not a method that is taken lightly as it can be seen that you are just idolizing ones self, so take time to listen and understand where everyone's point of view comes from, give reason to your individualism in a positive manner.

13

Keeping Communication Open

When in doubt, shout it out. Communication is a fortifying stronghold in the world that surrounds us, from the youngest child learning to cope peacefully with other children to our elders getting through each day. Communication is the biggest and most important way that we can go about providing each other a means to make a day worthwhile; it allows us to express ourselves in movements, actions or in words. Most prefer that someone listen to what we have to say and then have an equal or greater response to as things flow but occasionally we get the petty answer that lingers in our mind with "did they just say that?" or "What does that even mean?" In being individuals everyone has their own way of communicating to one another and search for other means of completing their own rings of a conversation with someone else just as easily. This can be fairly easy or complex depending on the person that you are talking to or dealing with, some people cannot handle a deep seated conversation because they have never grown to learn in that way or you may find yourself listening to someone that has much higher experience or intellectual level that now makes you feel as though you are dumbfounded. This is where the barriers need to be broken down and reformed into open air, because we all wish to be broadcast of our thoughts, it just becomes more of to what extent we do so with others. There are times when you may find someone just needs a moment to be alone for his or her own clarification and you feel the need to talk because a subject is fresh on the mind; then comes the idea that we can't always just talk about something right then and there because it may end up creating a new issue with personal handling of such ties. There are many times I so want to vent to the world any and all frustrations but choose not to do so directly but indirectly so that I can hopefully get what I need to say out without the dissolution of my own words, especially when you don't want to be misconstrued in what is being said. Believe it or not what you say right now is heard, and though your intent may have been a whole different idea; it may not have been taken in as the way it was intended. Learning to listen and truly listen is hard; everyone has opinions, variation in points of view in the conversation can cause chaos that was unforeseen or unexpected. Try listening and responding directly to that which is being addressed and give truthful responses, and if you don't have or know what to say then it is ok to not say anything minus giving acknowledgement that the other person was heard. Just don't wait to long because silence is deafening and anything else being said about your dealings or conversations can haunt your own thoughts or envisioning of why did the conversation go that way. I am horrible writer, probably one of the worst people to try and relate through text; but I try to as best as possible, though preferably talking is more of a strongpoint, since hearing the tones in your voice and echoes of my own words makes it easier to relay to what is actually happening or give a clearer ideology. Of course there is always the talking from the side bar or off the menu conversations that we manage to hear or talk about even if we aren't involved, here is where trouble can occur since first person is accurate to the account of which is being related. Though it can be difficult to avoid try to ignore the whimsical or the ill willed because they will fill your ears with lies or their own versions of how something is where you really are just in need of reality. Communicate as much as possible with those you love and cherish in your life and keep the roads as clear as possible to hopefully bring about a greater relationship and value to situations they may need attention too or you may have as well.

14

To Adore

Admire the great achievements your loved one has accomplished in their days. It could be something small, like they cleaned the house, or fixed the car; to something so much more like a great award or goal that you had been planning together for a long time. Bring with you the joy of their success and be proud of the many things they do, you in your own way may not see their it as a great thing that have done for some reason, however, anything that a person does from the simplest act to the most strenuous goals obtained can be seen with admiration. I commonly find myself bragging about my wife's achievements to friends, "my wife made the most delicious meal I have ever eaten, I ate three platefuls, so good." Or "my baby just fixed a thousand headsets in like three days, that's awesome." How you see things should be this way, you should admire the achievements of your loved one, and in doing so admire them. Admire them for the way they are, look, smell, feel, and as they desire. I know you cannot always read the other persons mind but when they ask you something like "do I look good in this, or how's this look?" Speak from your heart, "baby, you look fabulous, I think you are amazingly sexy." Now if something doesn't look right be honest, "No, that doesn't look very nice maybe try something else." I have listened to how my own father has described things to me and in turn it has taught me that when you admire your loved one and be definitive you should not look upon them with disgrace for any reason. This hurts so far beyond some random person saying something negative, cause you are the one they are most curious to hear from, so learn to show them a greater means in your descriptions. If your companion struggles with their perception of self, whether weight, personality or looks; give them your reasoning with admiration being part of natural speech. An example of this is your loved one thinks they are overweight, and you are concerned for their health as well, so in turn kindly say: "hey honey, it's a beautiful day outside, would you like to take a stroll with me around the block for some fresh air?" the littlest choice of mannerism can make a major difference. "Darling, I am concerned for your health, when you lay at rest I listen to your breathing and sometimes it sounds as though you are struggling, I would like to know if you would join me in an exercise because I am worried for our health." It is ok to use your words of admiration and caring to benefit both of your lives in a positive way especially if health or safety is involved. If one day you cannot find something to admire of your lover, then you aren't really looking at them for the person you love. You are not blind to these things but if when you love someone there are but a million things you will see and find in your partner that is worth admiring. My wife taught our son to tie his shoes, I always have used a complex way that he didn't quite understand so she took the time to show him a way I had never seen before; and in doing so I noticed she does it all the time with her shoes. She then not only showed him the way tie them and he now is very proficient at it, but I admired the craftiness and the fact she took time to aid even further, she even took some time to show me how to do this new method as well. Yes, admire the person or people that you cherish most; everything about someone is priceless and should be very precious to you.

15

Recognition

Pillsbury doughboy loves to be tickled in his belly, as do I. As burly and monstrous a man I am, like a little school-girl when tickled.... isn't it funny the things about someone you learn and come to find out. In some relationships the other person is very open and forward about their life, with things they have done in the past or stuff that they wish to do, whether simple or very complex. Ha ha, he likes to be tick-led... constantly we find a new thing to discuss or understand about one another that can be held true and given thought to keep hold of or disperse with a grain of salt. This is the choice of recognizing the other person for the type of being to where and which they have come from. Hey, some people choose not to be so open in their walks of life which is ok, time then is what will make the change and once comfortable expression follows; fortunately, my wife and I have shared everything about ourselves that really needs to be shared, sometimes even things that maybe shouldn't have been said but our comfort level has always been very high with each other. With this said, sometimes those things that are shared can rear up in a thought but not for the better; other times the recollection of discussions will help a situation that you both are now facing. Being open with one another is like laying concrete for the path you wish to walk together, solid and firm underneath you, you clearly know them as they know you for the real people you both are. "Pst, by the way, I can be a complete asshole." Personally, I have experienced a lot of jacked up stuff, not an excuse but so have many others in life that cause slight personality changes. Opening that door and letting the ones you care for know is essential in not only helping yourself realize an issue but also to recognize how to be better for them. I woke up covered in sweat, shaking and in tears. I am not alone, others have seen or heard horrible things as well. This is our life, sometimes it comes forth through recollection other times we blank out it to ensure we protect ourselves in an internal shell. In a relationship that you and your loved one have or are still building upon, it is important to allow them to see you for you and explain some of your difficulties. To understand your fears as their own and theirs as your own gives more of each other to be embraced for the person that you both are. As I have said earlier, I was not faithful to my first wife a few times, so one of my greatest fears in my eyes has become that my new wife would be un-faithful to me for some reason. It is a shared fear; she has expressed her concern of this as well with her knowing of my past relationship. So equally the concern was placed on the table; my side coming from what I have done and why, hers from me being her husband and not wishing that I did the same as I did before. Why? You may ask has this become a factor in our lives, because we need to know the other persons feelings about such issues, about how we as lovers learned from the mistakes we may have made and therefore grow to not fall into that which we fear of most. She loves the fact I am ticklish, it's silly but it's a fact. It's me. She loves to dress nice and look pristine, and this is how she is. You know if you see the person before you, have listened to where they come from and where they have been you are in a good place together. They may share something as you may as well that is very hard to accept easily, however, no matter it is that is shared be open and willing to love all of them, even if any mistakes have been made. Loving them fully and looking not at their past but at the person standing before you will allow you to share in life a much greater compassion for one another. These will also aid in times of need that come about giving way to help work through any trials faced. To be one; one heart, one spirit and one soul shared.

16

But What If?

UNDEFINDED - What in the hell is that crap? We all have those days, or those subjects that kind of hit you like a ton of bricks periodically. Hey, you never know how much of you can actually withstand the random crappiness unless this happens to you directly. I have stood before the man several times, uh yes; I am not always a good angel, and was trialed for stuff I did and stuff I didn't do, either way I stood there, and always ending up accepting whatever was handed to me. Not that I didn't fight at all, I sure as hell battled with grace and wittiness being pissed about some things, standing my ground hard. If I received punishment, I took it with tears of pain but never a breaking will, always withstand that which hurts most. Strides in life are not taken by just enduring heavy winters alone; they are in leaps of faith toward a greater common goal for us all. In such being said, when anything happens that cannot be described take many moments to recognize why, and what it truly is that is happening in and around you. Clarification as to the being you are, always believe that the undefined does come eventually; the answers may already be there for you and you are just struggling to put the pieces together one by one. If this is an issue within a relationship that you are piecing together ask for assistance, for their help in recognizing a problem or issue occurring with hopes that they are willing to be on the same page. That undefined situation could just be that it is that way to you, and they may have all the answers or visa versa. Some people say 'life outside the box" sorry, they are mentally incapable of reality, the box is life itself, it's what's inside the box that is different for everyone. Therefore, finding someone else's cube that matches yours entails making the undefined into what is defined. Not that being defined is how we all feel we need to be but in the structure of our own body and mind we should be defined. I define myself as proud, strong, intelligent, sexy and powerful... my wife defines me as a soft, gentle, loving; yet overbearing asshole. The common ground in this is that my definition of myself fits into the last part of her definition of me. Does this make for the undefined? No, because as we define ourselves, others will define us as well to how they perceive us. So when you happen to face the undefined however it comes about, seek out for a definitive answer. There always is one.

17

Roller Coaster

Le plaisir et la tristesse. Great plays and acts have been performed under these principles, for whatever reason we as humans feed upon the happiness or misery of someone else consistently. Wherever it has been written down there is never a story of pure happiness somewhere they all have a moment of sadness. It's like the ups and downs of our relationships. Not that we would wish for our relationships to have sad times by any means, but we all face different things parts of life which give this roller coaster affect. It may be work, school, social, or personal things that make it one messed up ride for those involved. On the bright side of things, today is today; you can change the way you feel about this moment or right now. Express this to your loved one let them know that you are sad or happy. Not only are you letting how you feel out but also now you are showing them that they have an opportunity to either share in your joy or give to sorrows to what you need. Be receptive the same of their days, the ride they may be on. My favorite reaction to my being upset is someone telling me to get over it… really?

 I carried a friend for over a mile once, bleeding out of his wrist and his head, the blood covered us continually but I still ran. I stitched the wounds as best I could for I was scared that I might lose him that day. Thankfully we eventually reached a medical facility to which I fought with him to keep him conscious and breathing through his vomits and blood… He suffers from short-term memory failure now, which he is dealing with on his own. I still remember that day like yesterday, my sadness comes that I was not faster, that I was not able to keep him safe to begin with and that he has a new problem that he faces every day. Am truly happy that he is alive and doing well now, but it constantly makes me think I did not do enough for him that day. I was told to get over it, he is ok… yes, he is very well off now but the sadness has dwelled within me for years. This is not the first time I have saved someone's life, it has happened before and yet in the joy of their surviving for whatever reason I still find sorrow for believing there could have been more done. You will never know the extent of your friends, or loved ones pains unless you ask or assist them in their troubles. Something's are very hard for a person, losing a loved one, a child, a best friend; these are very sad things, so inquire as to what you can do to help them in at least finding some happiness to their losses. Feed their soul with your joys and be enriched through love and caring for one another. The shallowest person still has deep emotion; they can be laughing outside and pained heavily on the inside. We all share a common ground with one another by that there are moments of happy and sad, but it is how we can associate with others throughout our lives that

make us alive and receive joy, even from sorrow.

18

Caring Abstract

To everyone that says they don't give a shit. Liar. If you didn't give a shit then why in the world did you listen to begin with, why did you even step foot into my life if this is your way of thinking. There must have been something you gave a shit about enough to become involved. Kind of gross, I don't really want your feces, but hey, you listened to me so far and so why did you even come around? Interest and curiosity can be placed on everyone in some manner of fashion. "I saw this pretty girl, she was chatting with her friends, and I wanted to see if I could persuade her my way." Also as "Holy cow, did you see that over there it was insane." Then people look... the grass is always greener so I am told, but so far I have yet to find a person that can say this is true, we all have our own defect. Knowing that everyone is messed up shouldn't make you less curious but always keep in mind that there may be more than what you really see or are being told. "Yo Dave, this chick is banging bro, has got everything I am looking for." Except three weeks later comes the "man, this chick is dumb as hell, and dude, she has got some serious problems dog." Eh, well, you took the interest; you had the curiosity so why not help her? Now you are in this relationship, find her for who she is not just because you thought she was gorgeous. Maybe I am trying to justify a little much here, cause not eve-rything can be helped with everyone, but if this is the person that you are looking at making your life partner, take a step back for a second from yourself and truly get to know the other person. There may be a lot of things that you share in common with them, and others you don't. That is ok if some things are not equal throughout your discussions; this is how we learn to relate to others better. Don't take me for granted cause curiosity did kill the cat. Be that of which you are, but displace this with that of the other person. If you cannot manage to get over yourself, then why the hell are you looking around to find someone else anyway? Misery loves company? Here is where you can really learn if you have grown up or not, biting into fruit that has no flavor just color or take time to fertilize the ground around it, tenderly handle it's growth so it ripens to a rich and full taste. I have used the aspect of personality defects as a trade for other things in life but with that, how could you as a person look at yourself to be proper if you are just gluten for the weakness you have in yourself. Back to original statement, 'I don't give a shit." Well, if you still don't then you don't appreciate that which you have in life or those you meet, then why the hell should anyone try to appreciate yours.

19

Smile

Three words: Live, Love, Laugh. Why not? Tomorrow I may not wake up, as if it really matters. Every day isn't going to be fabulous, hell some days might feel so much worse than others. Live each day to your best, love with the compassion of your heart, and laugh to the echoes of joy to the world around you. Can you see? It won't matter if I die then, cause life will go on, love will go on and laughter will be around. Not that I wish to die by any means, but this is how I see it when I get to the end of the day, that the day may have sucked horrendously but inside each day all of these are somehow found, through others or by myself. It's the kindle that lights the fire but it's the air around that keeps it going. Do not believe that you are alone, this is never true; you may feel this way, but you are not. If no one else in this world sees you, I do. Not like we are buddies that kick it on the weekend, but that you should know there is someone that cares always. That embraces the life that you have and everything you are. Nightfall hits hard to the ones that feel alone, the fall of the sun breaches their inner most fears and torments. Never a moment will pass that there isn't something worth so much less to life itself than you, not to be mistaken as self centered minding, but that a mental reality is that we all can find these three wonderful things daily. So live each day knowing that this is your day, and the people you share it with are parts of your life. Love, not everyone has found their love but love can be something we love to do; I love getting whooped on by my wife in Phase 10. Laugh—ha ha, is not a laugh, find something that brings laughter to your heart; I laugh just thinking about all the piggy back rides I have given to my wife, and jumping with her on my back as she grips tighter around my neck. These don't have to be a right now thing, they can be things that you remember and think about from your past. See your life as a true gift, a blessing, and most cherished by not only you, but by those around you cause your life is important.

20

Always Learning

Teachers are really cool people. They have dedicated themselves to working with our children as well as sometime had worked with us to give us knowledge and hopefully lead us to success. I am not a teacher, I have instructed many and through instruction given many the opportunity to grow. Teaching is different; it is the insight to visit your own learning with a great passion for the students like no other. I did thoroughly enjoy my position but was not able to aid everyone the same. It's uncanny how when we go through schooling, most people try to interrupt or disperse of what is being taught to them as if it does not matter at all. It is natural to be disobedient in some way but why the course that could lead to so much more? This is where that moment of truth first comes to light; did we really listen as we were taught? Most of the time it is a delayed response because we fool ourselves into thinking we are right. So, did we seek the guidance that they have provided for us? Who really knows but ourselves, and in this you should find a real answer to the balance between knowledge and enlightenment. They are quite different; my mother-in-law is so much more enlightened than I. She is quite exquisite in her way of describing things and providing true care to those around her. She is more educated as well, but I listen to her speak to me more so since she knows more to life than I have learned yet but wish to encompass. Teachers can come in all forms and walks of life, they surround us in each day, and even if not always given notice we should listen for they may change you and give you opportunity to become more advanced in some way. It is possible that the one that is teaching you are the one you love as well. Let them, even if it hurts or you want to struggle because of your own opinions, stop, breathe, listen and try to quell to what they are saying to you. It may be something simple as to how to make pancakes the right way, or more complex as to finding greater means to a shared enlightenment. Nothing is always easy, if that was the case then anyone can do anything right now… you can anything you put your mind too, but I am saying unless you went to school for half a decade, you can't just cut someone's head open and do brain surgery. How we go about describing to one another in this manner does play a part, if you are mad, don't try to teach the other person of what they did or do that makes you mad. Try to choke on your own spit for a minute, it's kind hard; I have been trying to do it myself, sucks, you got to build up some saliva just to even attempt it. Now after trying for a while, try to be open to their thoughts, and hopefully they will be willing to receive yours. Who is the teacher in your relationship should not be one or the other; it should be mutual, shared thoughts and ideals to which you both can be receiving of more. Be open to being taught no matter where the teaching comes from.

21

Speaking as One

"The fires of hell will consume your soul." "Um…. no bitch, you better recognize, I eat souls." Powerful we are, the words that we say can be used in a manner to strike fear, just sound silly or justifying to an extent. In your relationship, you must learn to speak of your own manners to each other. In words, and in actions do we see each other and develop this language. This is a higher language than that which you use for other people in your life. They come to sense your emotions and feeling, it becomes a mutual identification. We have devoted ourselves to speaking this language to one another as to aid in our relationship in times of joy and not joy. Ever have a friend blame some bad gas on you? Ever have your love do it? Very different, we are appalled or redirect this to our friend, where with our love we may crinkle a little, or just let it pass. Everyone will react different to my example there; I make no promise that your significant other wont point and say something back to you. However it is the difference that I am talking about. This language that has become something for you two alone, now if you don't know what I am talking about still well then you may need to look for the differences. One can only hope that their partnership has been very equal in conceptions and ideals to where everything becomes simple enough in motion. I see my wife come home; I can tell if her day was good or rugged. She may ask for a back massage, but by that time I already know that she needs it and have already started on her feet. It's our love that teaches us to be receptive of this language, and speak it equally with our partner. Even in translation, others will see this language being spoken fluently between you two and can notice changes in demeanor or actions as they flow about. It's as though being in a higher state of being with one another, to where sometimes there is not even a need for words. There will be still be moments when our common voice is heard over our equal voice and at that point you may need a jump-start, but once that motor fires off, it will keep running.

22

Passing Judgements

"Who the hell are you to judge?" Interesting, this can be a correct and incorrect statement at the same time. You may see it as they are judging you first and foremost. Lots of times if I get told this I kind of question as to why they said this to begin with, cause if we are seeing an action or hearing something not right in our own upbringing then yes there is an internal thought on how this should have or could have gone. Especially when it's direct, it directly affects you, something you are doing or most important your relationship somehow. Now, judging others is wrong, they need to make mistakes and learn themselves and no matter much we would like to see otherwise or protect them from their own downfall it's better to listen or observe while waiting to give a reason to your concern for their methodology. Trust me, I have failed at this a lot and in many stupid ways too. How I know I failed is that instead of judging what's going on or what is being said with clear and sound mind, I have looked to the person or people causing the problem. In that aspect there is more of anger some side that arises when blame is placed from judging others, or some amount of pain induced if misjudging a project, like watching my uncle shoot a nail through his foot with his nail gun. Sometimes this isn't bad, a child steals from a store; you punish them for the act and in this you have judged them for their disobedience to social law. MORE, being the word of indulgence, when placed in a position of power where judgments of right and wrong can change lives or end them. The capability to have a loving partner, and friendships, without judgments becomes more to be desired. The tasking is that we can do as our day requires and return to life with our partner without judging anything around you or them for something they may have done that you disagreed with.

23

Perfect

Perfection is nowhere to be found no matter how hard you look. Accept this. There is no one alive that is perfect; there is no one that is going to be perfect. This doesn't mean that you can't or don't have the perfect person for you. Some people do lie and say they are perfect people with absolutely nothing wrong with them at all…. Sorry but that just means you are a liar and actually not perfect by any means. Interestingly though, all my friends will tell you that I swear to god my wife is perfect. She is to me; in my eyes, my wife is perfect, that's all that matters. We would all love to find perfection, but now you have tried to undermine thought, physics, emotion and reasonability. Being of sound mind will make it easier to understand how you view your relationships and how to see what you find as perfection. Is there really an issue with finding someone that is perfect for you but maybe not for everyone else? I can tell you right now that a lot of people don't like me for being an alpha male. To be honest, I love being a giant teddy bear, hugs and kisses as much as possible... Most people will never see that through my hardened shell; but that's on the outside, it's what I show the world as I go about the day. It is funny, because my wife caught on pretty quickly when we first met, she saw the outside me being a mean guy to a bunch of people, but then she took time to really meet me as the man I am... She is perfect in my eyes, and I to hers. When you are seeking or finding your partner, you are looking for a perfect someone the one that sparkles in your eyes and gives endless joy to your heart. This is not a dream to have or to wish to obtain, but you have to really look at people for who they truly are. That bright star in your world will come through meaning, and intuition. They as people or you yourself may not be perfect by any means, but seeing to the perfection that you have found in your love one will guide you through every moment together with each other. They will enjoy that you find this aspect in them, as you will appreciate them more and more in return.

24

Life Choices

Today in the lifestyle we choose have the opportunity to reflect upon the lifestyle that we wish for. You may be the type of person that has run chaotically through the world with wind at your back and nothing to stop you but death itself, or the person who takes consideration for the life they lead and how it may change them as they grow. These things can be the greatest lessons or the biggest downfalls, but it would only be as you wish them to be, if you don't adhere to your own mental capacity for civil life you may be outcast and slandered for that which you did not control. Not to say that you may not have attempted to make a difference in your life for better or worse, but how is it if you go about running around without the idea that something may hurt you or change you later, that you will know what truly is the right way? In seeing the chaotic hell raiser that I have been I notice the change as well, and so do others. The people I offended or hurt see that as I grow more each day, I learn new lessons on the man that I wish to be. No I am not there yet, as most of us are not and may take a little while to find that person but listening and taking in consideration for that which you were aids heavily toward making yourself more than what once was. Does that mean you should be perfectly obedient to every rule and adhere to being perfect? Is that even possible? I don't think so, there is always something about everyone that isn't going to be exact and may cause them to be indifferent to society or social groups. You could just say, I am one of a kind, or plainly I am different. Unless you are a science experiment of cloning, then we all are going to be different. So it is natural to do random stuff or be found wanting of that which we may not really need right then, this is how it is, if we were dogs it would be easy. Eat, poop, pee, sleep, play, repeat… but this is not so, we're of a higher thought process; however, this also means that others may choose a side of negativity for that which you have done and use it against you in some way. Can this be fixed? Yes it can, but it takes time and warding yourself to show there is a change within you for the better. Never the less we are all creatures of habit in a lot of ways, hopefully each of us realizes the bad habits or tendencies that we have before this repeats itself and you are right back where you started. Only you can make the change, only you can repeal the past and find repentance from that which you have done. No one else can walk your path and make the choices for you.

25

Love

"I love you" - this should be the ultimate thing you say to your partner, and not just to say it. It should have meaning from your heart, your mind and soul. These words should be a pure reflection of the way you feel about your partner. There is no mistake in when you say this to someone if you really mean it, there is no taking back what you have said. When you say these three words, your body should light up with joy from inside and out, and your loved one should feel the emotions mutually. Many times have I heard my own friends say these words to a girl to get in their pants or hook up for a little while, just to push them away at the first sign of another partner, or chance at another partner. I am glad that my own mother has taught me that when you love someone and only when you really love them do you tell them this. I fully understand that some people will say it and there is not a response or there is some delay where they are only saying it as a repeat to make the other person feel better. This should not be that way, when embracing the fact that you are in love with someone then it is easy to say it and let your heart pour to them. I don't wish for people to just say this because they feel they have too… the words "I love you" should always bare truth to your sense of feelings and affection for one another. There are two types of love though, which maybe these words are used inappropriately to describe both, and we should understand the difference. I love my mother, even though we have had our moments of not liking each other for whatever reason, I love her as the woman she is, for all that she has done for me and all her caring. This is so very different from the love that I have for my wife, I love her with passion, endearment, and with all of my heart. You may say they still seem similar for the most part. No it is different, when I look at my mother I see a woman that loves me unconditionally for that I am or once was; yet when I look upon my wife, I see the most beautiful, and amazing person that I have ever been blessed to have in my life, I adore her. I love her, and I am in love with her. Does this always hold the same value for everyone you meet, no they may have their own reasoning or thoughts on love itself; but they should be pure in the ways that they love someone as well. Hopefully everyone finds a great love and has so many wonderful blessings to keep their love flowing strong. A fool can be bantered to what they desire through such words of endearment being used freely without recognizing the purpose or even feeling their heart. So listen to the beats of your heart when it comes to your own feelings, and make sure to truly open your eyes to take in the returning feel of that affection. If the love and compassion is shared the sound should resonate through you their words, not because you want to hear them, but because there is real meaning behind them.

26

The Most Important Step

Marriage obviously is a great step between two people. This is when your loved one and you have decided to become one. To share each other's days, nights, happiness, sadness, laughter or sorrow. To share the life with another person who knows you as you them, understands your strengths and weaknesses, whom feels that this is the person I want to spend my life with. Got to love seeing newly weds, so overjoyed and playful running around chaotically as they try to rebalance their lifestyle's and methods of living. It's like watching meteorites collide and reform into bigger ones. A sound marriage has nothing to hide, nothing that cannot be shared with the other person even if it may cause disarray for a little while. In taking their hand and becoming one, you have accepted that person for who they are, they have been, and wish to be. Things happen for a reason, we meet someone, we share about ourselves, we grow to love each other and we become one. I may be wrong in my thinking, but in a marriage, we are not individuals but a conglomerate of divinity. Who can say that their marriage is all just one sided, that they have control over everything and the other person shouldn't open their mouth or have any thoughts at all? If you are that person, I suggest a book called *Secrets of Great Marriages* by Charlie and Linda Bloom. There is equality in all of us, she shouldn't have to wash the dishes or vacuum or clean just because you say so. "I had a horrible day at work but I don't want to tell him cause I don't want a pity party." Ok, the moment of truth, it's alright to share what's going in your day- maybe forewarn them with "I had a pretty rough day today but it I made it" then lead to the crap that made your day bad, you will get a different response. In turning the tides over by letting your spouse know that it sucked but that you are ok is a way for them to stop their own traveling to protection mode, especially men whom in a marriage defend their woman like a Spartan. I know I have reversed the order there in which I am talking about actions within a marriage because women seem to have a different mindset then men, we can be fairly ignorant and it's a lot easier to say this to a man: "get off your ass and aid your partner around the house and show her that you are willing to share in these projects because she is important to you and you would like to give her some time to relax." Simplicity is nice sometimes. Marriage is such a beautiful thing but can be a very hard thing as well, it will always be easier when both people can see each other for the one they love and as the their one and only love. Not saying that you may not like your spouse at that moment, from time to time you may dislike the things they do or the way they are acting. This is where love and cherished memories you share and have had come with great pleasures of your matrimonial vows. "I promise to be true to you in good times and bad, to have and to hold, for better or for worse, for richer or poorer, in sickness and in health, till death do us part." Clearly stated, I will give you all of me as you do I because we are one and we are of togetherness to give each other a more meaningful life. It is with these vows that those of us that walk this path look to more reasons in life and love to give more of ourselves to our partner. There are always going to be things that may occur that are not favorable to either person but this is where our individuality and our unification become that of a higher meaning; as an individual you will have your own thoughts or ways to deal with a problem, then as a unified body there may be a different aspect or reasoning that you may not have thought of. Where the X and Y-axis come together is where we see each other, yes I did just use a mathematical reference but if a graph was designed solely on each person's relationship it surely would never be a straight line. This is where your faithfulness comes into it's own fashion of thinking objectively, I love him/her with all my heart, I promised to give my all, I will help them to reach our common ground and not fail. Marriage, it is the unification of two people, a longing to be part of someone else's life and them yours; cherish it, for it is a true blessing.

Never let yourself forget these lines:

"I will love and honor you all the days of my life."

There will always be people that come up with excuses to a lot of the thing written here don't judge for that which you may not know or are willing to negate so easily. I personally have come to a point in life where it doesn't matter what others think of me, aside from my wife and children. I am an asshole in that respect; however I am a good man, I am a great father, a good friend, and endless lover. I know me, no matter how the day goes; in the end I have clarity of myself. I wish that were true of everyone, but we all are learning and growing together for the better.

www.ingramcontent.com/pod-product-compliance
Lightning Source LLC
Chambersburg PA
CBHW031243280526
45784CB00004B/1705